30 WAYS
A FATHER CAN BLESS
HIS CHILDREN

JOHN TRENT, PH.D.

30 Ways a Father Can Bless His Children
Copyright © 2015 John Trent
Aspire Press is an imprint of
Rose Publishing, LLC
P.O. Box 3473
Peabody, Massachusetts 01961-3473 USA
www.hendricksonrose.com

*Special thanks to Kari Trent and Tamara Love
for their assistance in making these books possible.*

All scripture quotations, unless otherwise indicated, are taken from the New American Standard Bible®, Copyright © 1960, 1962, 1963, 1968, 1971, 1972, 1973, 1975, 1977, 1995 by The Lockman Foundation. Used by permission.

Scripture quotations marked (NIV) taken from the Holy Bible, New International Version®, NIV®. Copyright ©1973, 1978, 1984, 2011 by Biblica, Inc.™ Used by permission of Zondervan. All rights reserved worldwide. www.zondervan.com The "NIV" and "New International Version" are trademarks registered in the United States Patent and Trademark Office by Biblica, Inc.™

Scripture quotations marked (ESV) taken from The Holy Bible, English Standard Version Copyright © 2001 by Crossway Bibles, a publishing ministry of Good News Publishers.

Printed in the United States of America
August 2018, 2nd printing

CONTENTS

WHAT THE BLESSING IS

IT'S BEEN SAID—and I agree—that every child in every home deserves to know that someone is crazy about them. Beyond that, every child in every home deserves to know that *Jesus* is crazy about them as well. But how do you make that a reality for your child? How do you go "all in" for every child in your home in a way that can make all the difference for them today and tomorrow?

This book is all about being the kind of father who communicates that kind of wild "I'm crazy about you" love and commitment for his kid—not the kind of unhealthy attachment that smothers a child, breeds selfishness, or blocks the child's growth towards independence and responsibility, but a gift you can give your children that empowers and unleashes them to be free to serve others, gain personal strength, and grow in responsibility—a gift that helps them not only see your love but also embrace the truth that with God's love, they can do and be more than they even dreamed or imagined.

IN THIS VERY CHALLENGING WORLD, YOUR CHILD DESPERATELY NEEDS YOUR BLESSING!

Having even one person in our life who really believes in us that way can get us moving towards a special future, towards purpose and hope and acceptance. What's more, that one person can get and keep us pointed towards God's love and his best through every new season of life.

That is especially true in the early years of life. We need just one person in our home who really sees us as incredibly valuable, who really believes in us and tells us that we have a unique set of God-given talents, strengths, and abilities that he's put in our life—strengths he can use for good someday.

That kind of "I'm all in" love can become a tipping point for a child, a way of shifting your son or daughter past all the challenges they'll face in real life, all the unkind words they'll hear, all the messages of "You can't do that" from people who won't believe in them.

And, Dad, you need to be that person: a man wise enough and caring enough to give each of your sons and daughters your blessing. Not that their mother's blessing isn't important. It's crucial as well. (In fact, I've written another book for mothers to use in giving the blessing to their sons and daughters.) But every dad has the unique opportunity to show each of his children that they are incredible and that they are an incredible gift from God as well.

In this very challenging world, your child desperately needs your blessing!

An Old Testament Example

In the Old Testament, we are introduced to the practice of fathers passing on a blessing to their children. A well-known biblical account of the giving of the blessing is found in the Genesis story of Jacob and Esau. (Look up Genesis 27 if you'd like to read it yourself).

Jacob and Esau were fraternal twin sons of Isaac. All their lives, each son sought after his father's blessing. But in this home, only one son would receive the blessing, and the other would cry out when he found he had missed it forever, "Bless me, even me also, O my father!" (Genesis 27:34).

That same thing, I'm convinced, takes place in every home today.

In every home, with every father, there is a choice set before that man: a choice to bless his children—to communicate that incredible gift of unconditional love and acceptance that his children long for from the earliest years forward—or to actively or passively withhold the blessing from his children, leading to a lifetime of emotional hurt.

The words may be different from Esau's terrible cry in the Bible—"Do you have only one blessing, my father? Bless me, even me also, O my father" (Genesis 27:38)—but I hear those kinds of heartbreaking words echoed in my counseling office week after week from a now-grown son or daughter, someone who still longs for that gift that was never given, that blessing that never came from their father.

And that's so wrong and unnecessary! There are so many times I wish I could turn back the years and sit down with that father who's chosen to withhold the blessing, to share with him why it's so important and explain why God blessed us and how we can, in turn, bless others, starting with our own family. And in most cases, what I'd likely find out is that he just didn't know! He just simply didn't know how important it was to bless his son or daughter—and too often, that's because he never got the blessing himself!

If you did get the blessing growing up as a child, then you'll get the concepts that follow right away. You lived them. They'll remind you of the many similar ideas you experienced up close and personal from your own father as you got the blessing. They'll motivate you to do what you've experienced. But if you're like me and you didn't get the blessing growing up, this book is crucial for you. You need to know that water can rise above its own level. You can reverse the curse, even if it's generations long. You can learn what it means to bless others. You'll see how in so many small ways, you can hand that incredible gift of the blessing to your kids (and your spouse) and experience it yourself!

I really think I have the best job in the world. My day job is serving as the Gary Chapman Chair of Marriage and Family Ministry and Therapy at Moody Theological Seminary. The ministry part of that long title means I get to do seminars across the country and to teach Moody graduate students getting ready to head off to churches where they will teach parents and singles to bless and build up their families. But the other part of my job has to do with therapy. That's crucial too, as we equip the next generation of family pastors and Christian counselors. We teach them how to come alongside and encourage and build up those who didn't get the blessing, to help them move past the hurt and move towards hope and health. That is, people like me!

A Personal Example

I grew up in a single-parent home. My father chose to bail out on our family when I was two months old. (Actually, with my twin brother and older brother, there were three of us under the age of three when he left). We didn't grow up going to church on Sundays; we went to the library. Growing up, I never heard about the blessing in the Bible.

But without a doubt, what I was missing in my life and needed so much as a child and then as a young man was my father's blessing. Without it, I became incredibly angry with and distant from others. You might

> GOD PUT ONE MAN IN MY LIFE WHO MADE A CHOICE TO LIVE OUT THE BLESSING BEFORE ME.

call it attachment disorder today, if you were looking for a label. And while anger might have helped me in athletics, it ruined my relationships with others.

Yet I thank God that while I was in high school, he put one man in my life who made a choice to live out the blessing before me—to live it out with his own family first and then in front of a bunch of high school football players, including me and my brother. And it changed our whole family's life.

I didn't read about the blessing in the Bible or a Christian book. I saw it lived out by a six-foot-four former offensive tackle who showed up as our new Young Life leader.

Not only did I get to see Doug Barram bless his own family, but like Jesus blessing children who weren't his own, Doug was world-class at giving his blessing as well to a bunch of really hurting, really needy young men. And, again, it changed our lives!

I'm convinced that the greatest tool for evangelism that the church has today is a home filled with God's light and love—a home like Doug's where they knew how to live and give God's blessing. What I learned from Doug changed my life, and it can change your life too, especially if you've never received the blessing. And it's part of why I've written this book as well: to share with you that once you have Jesus' love inside you—even if you're like me and didn't come from the best of backgrounds—you can learn to give that incredible gift of the blessing to your children! You get to be the man who chooses life over death and who reverses the curse into blessing in his family!

But it all starts with a choice: a choice to bless. And it's a choice that God says will impact generations!

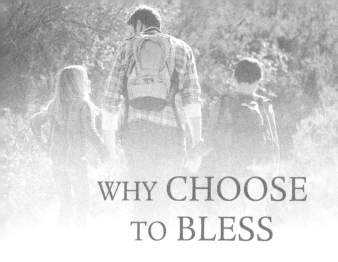

WHY CHOOSE TO BLESS

Life over Death, Blessing over Curse

In Deuteronomy, the Lord says to his people, "I call heaven and earth to witness against you today, that I have set before you life and death, blessing and curse. Therefore choose life, that you and your offspring may live" (Deuteronomy 30:19, ESV). That's one choice with two parts: (1) life over death, and (2) blessing over curse. In Scripture the word *life* means movement; things that are alive are moving towards someone or something. The word *death* means to step away. That's a word picture of your first choice as a father.

Are you going to step towards your son or daughter—with appropriate touch, with spoken words that attach high value, by picturing a special future for them and showing them your genuine commitment? Or are you going to choose to step away—because of work, because you just don't know how to bless them, or because you never got the blessing yourself?

SMALL THINGS COMMUNICATE GOD'S LOVE TO YOUR CHILDREN.

There is no middle ground. Your child will look back on your relationship with him or her when they've grown up, and they will know in their heart of hearts the answer to this question: *Did my father choose to step towards me or away from me?* No father is perfect. But each father has that choice set before him: to choose life over death, to step towards or to step away.

And know this: what keeps us choosing to step towards our son or daughter (and our spouse) is having made that first foundational choice for life in Christ! That's LIFE in all capitals!

The new life Jesus gives us when we choose him

gets us moving towards others in service, love, and commitment! The abundant life he offers us gives us his power and strength to keep moving towards our child in a positive way—even on those days (or seasons) when it's tough or difficult to do so or when we really feel like stepping away. Even if we ourselves never got the blessing growing up, we can change the pictures of our life story! Jesus promised us, "I have come that you might have life, and have it abundantly" (John 10:10). He gets us unstuck and moving towards him—and towards others!

So that's the choice set before you. Are you going to step towards or step away from the Lord? To step towards or away from your children? Your spouse?

Very soon, you'll learn thirty ways I stepped towards our children, ways that I've taught to fathers across the planet to bless their children as well. They're not the only thirty that count. You can adjust and even change every one. But you'll soon see that it's small things like these examples that you can draw on to communicate God's love to your children. In small but often unforgettable ways, you can say to them "I'm crazy about you" as you get moving towards your son or daughter. Amazingly, those small things over time create what we call a culture of the blessing in your home.

Two Word Pictures

In Scripture, the Hebrew word for *to bless* suggests two pictures. The first picture is that of bowing the knee. This doesn't mean we have to bow literally to our child! That would be a little strange and confusing to them in our culture! But it's a picture of our acknowledging—which bowing did in olden times and still does in some cultures—that we are in the presence of someone who's extremely valuable. In this case, it's our son or daughter who we've chosen to bless.

The second picture of blessing carries the idea of adding weight or value—like adding coins to an ancient scale. The greater the weight, the higher the value. Our actions towards our children should say, "You are valuable to me, and I choose to add to your life."

Think about how we bless the Lord. When we say that (or sing those words), we're really saying, "Lord, you're so valuable, I bow the knee before you." But then we add our praise to him. In short, when we bless a child, we're acknowledging in our heart that our child has great worth and value, and then we act on that choice to value them by adding to their life!

A Culture of Blessing

But what do we add to bless a child (or others)? As a father, you'll see there are five things, or elements, of the blessing that surface every time the blessing was given in Scripture. Amazingly, while God's Word was written centuries ago, those same five elements of the blessing are foundational in clinical research reflecting what makes healthy families!

Of course, the act of a father's giving of the blessing isn't just reserved for a once-in-a-lifetime momentous occasion. There were times in Scripture when the blessing was given at the end of a father's life, but you see other times when very young children were given the blessing! Jesus blessed young children that weren't his own. In fact, a father or mother in biblical times could bless their child *every day*. And you can pass on the blessing to your son or daughter in small ways every day as well.

In fact, it's all these small, specific, positive ways that can help you as a father create what we call a culture of the blessing in your home! Think about a culture like setting a thermostat in your home. Try living in Chicago in February and setting the thermostat at 20 degrees throughout the house. No matter where you go in that home, the atmosphere, or culture, communicates one thing: it's cold! Your whole focus isn't on relating to others or being free to do things inside; your focus is on getting warm! But now set the thermostat at 72 degrees and watch life warm up and the focus of your family go from what's missing (heat) to all the things you *can do* as a family! You've added life (movement) to the home, because you've changed the thermostat (or culture)! And when you create a culture of the blessing in the home, kids grow up knowing "I've got it! I've got my parent's blessing!" No searching for it all their life like too many children are forced to do. No focus on what's lost but on freedom to move towards God's best!

Here's an example from my own home to illustrate.

When Kari, our oldest child, was about five years old, we'd done many of the thirty things you'll see in this book to build into her life the blessing. But one night, she had "one of those nights" when it was really hard for her to go to sleep. We brought her water. Then a second glass of water, this time with ice cubes. Then there was the trip to the bathroom after all that water. Then a warm washcloth to soothe her. But at that point, it was obvious this was just becoming a game. That's when I told her, "That's it, Kari. No more getting out of bed. Period. We'll see you in the morning."

> YOU CAN POINT YOUR CHILDREN TOWARDS GOD'S BEST AND HIS BLESSING TOMORROW, EVEN IF YOUR FATHER NEVER GAVE YOU THE BLESSING!

Kari didn't get out of bed again. But she did something that my wife and I have never forgotten: from down the hall, Kari yelled out to us, "'Night, Mom! 'Night, Dad! And don't forget to bless me in the morning!"

Cindy and I just looked at each other and the feelings were overwhelming. Neither Cindy nor I grew up in a home where we had that kind of certainty and love and blessing. Cindy came from an alcoholic home, and I came from a single-parent home. And neither one of us had grown up in a Christian home. Yet here was Kari (finally) heading off to sleep, reminding us to have that gift waiting for her in the morning. Not a Christmas or birthday present. Something even more important to a child. She knew she had our blessing.

And this book can help you put that kind of unconditional love—that kind of "I got it!" deep-seated knowledge of unconditional acceptance—in the center of your son or daughter's heart. Something that can impact their life today and can point them towards God's best and his blessing tomorrow.

You can point your children towards God's best and his blessing tomorrow, even if your father never gave you the blessing!

BLESSING BASICS

The Five Essential Elements

Let's get more specific about just what we mean by the blessing, before we jump into these thirty you-can-do-this! examples coming up. The reason why is you'll see them pop up in the suggestions and examples that follow.

First, the blessing begins with a *meaningful touch*. The blessing continues with a *spoken message*, meaning you say or write out your blessing, so it is unmistakable. The third element of the blessing is how your words always express *high value*. Fourth, you imagine a *special future for your child*. And then these four attitudes and actions are lived out and demonstrated through an *active commitment* to see the blessing come to pass in your child's life. Each of these five elements contributes its own impact on your blessing.

Meaningful Touch

A *meaningful touch* was an important part of giving the blessing in the Old Testament. When Isaac blessed his son, he called him, saying, "Come near and kiss me, my son" (Genesis 27:26, ESV). Isaac's words "come near" actually translate as "come and embrace in a bear hug." Isaac believed he was speaking to Esau, who was more than forty years old at the time! Isaac sets an example of a father who didn't limit touch to his sons due to their age, an example fathers should pay attention to. The benefits of touch are enormous—physically, emotionally, and spiritually.

Spoken Message

A *spoken message* has the power to build up or tear down a child's worth and heart and are a big part of cementing your love and building a healthy attachment to your child. Can you remember words of praise that your father spoke to you? What about words of criticism? Our words hold great power, and the blessing acknowledges this through the spoken message. In the Bible, a blessing was invalid unless it was spoken. In the book of James, we see multiple pictures of the power of the tongue. The tongue is described as a bit that gives direction to a horse, a rudder that turns a ship, and a spreading fire (James 3:1–6). Each of these pictures shows us the potential of the tongue to build up or tear down. Will your tongue be one that encourages or belittles? Children desperately need to hear positive words spoken to them. The words of a father hold incredible weight in the heart of a child. Choose to speak words of blessing to your son or your daughter.

High Value

But what kind of words are we to speak or write down for our child? Those that communicate *high value*. To value something is to attach great importance to it. In blessing our children, we are choosing to ascribe great worth to them, acknowledging that they are valuable to the Lord and to us. This is important, even in times of difficulty with our children. Children push our buttons, try us emotionally, exhaust us physically, and often deplete us financially! But in the times when we may not feel the value of our sons and daughters, choosing to speak words of high value to them realigns our own perspective and encourages our children to see their value as well.

Special Future

With our *meaningful touch*, with our choice to use a *spoken message*, and by attaching words with *high value* to a child, we lay the foundation to help us picture a *special future* for our children as well. As we attach value to a person, we can see their potential and envision the great ways in which they might impact the world for Christ. Kids are literalists when it comes to hearing words that point them towards a special future or when they hear that they're a failure, pathetic, or a loser. By paying attention to the strengths your child exhibits, you can see how that sensitivity they show with other children today might make them a great counselor, teacher, or coach down the road. How that leadership talent today could be something that Jesus uses to help them change the world for the better tomorrow. Every person is gifted uniquely. How is your son or daughter gifted? How might their strengths benefit their relationships and future endeavors? Paint a picture with your words of your child's future and it can be, literally, unforgettable for them as they go through life.

Active Commitment

The last element of the blessing really seals the deal, as the one giving the blessing demonstrates an *active commitment* to see the blessing come to pass in that child's life. Words have to be accompanied by action. The blessing is not merely spoken but lived— even when it's hard. Giving the blessing to your child doesn't mean you don't discipline them. All kids are like you. Fallen. In need of a Savior. And in need of someone who loves them enough to say *no* at times, to point them down the right path, and to correct wrongs. But rules without a relationship is a great way to breed rebellion in a child's heart. The blessing gives you the platform to do discipline well, because your children know you love them deeply and care what direction their life is taking.

Dad, be intentional about connecting with and blessing your son or daughter today. And as you do, you will be adding layer after layer of love and acceptance into their life that they'll need and can draw strength from all their lives!

And you're not alone in doing this! The Lord honors those who seek him and depend on him for help. We're to be the spiritual trainers in our home (Deuteronomy 6:6–9). And we serve a great and mighty God who can keep us stepping towards our child, not stepping away.

Using this acronym is an easy way to remember all five elements:

B stands for "be committed" (active commitment)

L stands for "lovingly touch" (meaningful touch)

E stands for "express value" (high value)

S stands for "see potential" (special future)

S stands for "say it!" (spoken message)

You might consider posting this acronym on your fridge, on your bathroom mirror, or maybe by your desk computer—somewhere that you look regularly and can be reminded of your own desire to give the blessing to your son or daughter. Use it as a tool to check up on yourself and evaluate how you are doing with each element.

Show-and-Tell

So now you know what the blessing is and why it's so important to choose to bless your child's life. The rest of the book is show-and-tell.

Any teacher knows that show-and-tell can be even more powerful than just tell. So in the pages that follow, I want to show you thirty simple, practical ways that parents like you have used—and that I've used—to pass on the blessing to a child.

You certainly aren't limited to these thirty, but I hope they will act as a springboard for your efforts to pass on the blessing to your son or daughter. You will see that each suggestion incorporates a variety of the five elements of the blessing. Some focus on using spoken words. Others incorporate a meaningful touch or help you to picture a special future. In some of the examples and occasions discussed, you'll see where all five come together in one activity or suggestion! And, yes, some aspects of each blessing might be easier for you to give than others. But the cumulative result of implementing all five elements of the blessing will help your son or daughter in so many ways—emotionally, physically, spiritually.

You goal isn't to try and mark a checklist as you use each example. I want you to feel a sense of freedom, in that every attempt at passing on the blessing doesn't have to meet a list of must-do criteria. Nor does it have to result in the best evening ever or some huge emotional response from your child: "Oh, thanks, Dad, for spending time with me. I'll remember this all my life." What you're looking to do is choose to layer in the blessing—to create that 72-degree culture of caring, acceptance, commitment, and courage in your home. It's not about perfection or emotion or doing something just right. It is about jumping in and going all in on being a father who is going to *choose* to bless his son or daughter.

You'll see some everyday blessings you can do, and some blessings that are great when the whole family is gathered together. There are spiritual blessings that link your blessing with God's love and blessing. And I've included examples of how even when you're on the go or in the car, you can bless your child. There are blessings that help your children learn an important skill—like money matters—some character blessings, and finally, some blessings that help them understand their unique, God-given strengths. So use all these ideas as a jump start, a launching pad, that can get you into the habit of creating that culture of the blessing with your son or daughter.

Your kids may not cry out down the hall for you to bless them in the morning. But they will carry to bed—and carry in their hearts all their days—their father's blessing. *What a gift.* And what a joy and peace in your heart, knowing, *I wasn't perfect, but I did my best to bless my child.* And that begins with just simple blessings that you can do everyday, like the thirty examples here.

30 WAYS TO BLESS YOUR CHILDREN

1

20-Questions Blessing

 As we launch into our simple ideas for passing on the blessing, I want you to consider this question: Who is someone in your life who you felt genuinely took an interest when you spoke with them? Someone who really heard you when you talked? Can you picture someone like that from when you were a child?

I've had times when I've given more attention to a game on television or emails I was reading on the tablet I was holding than really listening to or seeing my children. But one thing I did learn to do that was so easy and became such a help in my communicating with them started with a tennis ball and 20 Questions!

It happened one day when I picked up our oldest daughter from school. As usual, I asked Kari the same question I asked every day: "So how'd your day go at school?" and I got the same response: "Fine."

But then I saw a tennis ball that was in the cup holder.

I handed Kari the tennis ball and said, "OK, here's the deal. Before we get home, I'm going to ask you twenty questions. I'll hold the ball and ask you the question; then I hand you the ball. When you're done answering the question, you hand the ball back to me. We've got to get going if we're going to get to twenty questions, so here's the first question."

And thus started our version of 20 Questions, which became a great way to really listen to and bless our children—and others!

Little did I know that not settling for just a "fine"

answer could open up the doors to talk about so many hurts, challenges, and dreams. That doesn't mean that every question I asked them had to be serious or opened the floodgates of communication. But after a few "fines" or some other short answers, there would be that one question that hit a nerve. Then we'd be off to really communicating about their hurts or dreams or concerns or fears or goals.

We rarely got to asking twenty questions by the time we got home, but there were times when I'd literally pull over the car to keep the discussion going. Or before we opened the garage door at home, Kari or Laura would ask, "Can we keep passing the ball?"

I'd usually start off with a silly question like, "If we could drive right now to any place in Phoenix and get a snack, where would we go?" Or, "If you were an animal just for one day, which animal would you be?" But those fun questions led to other questions: "So if you could help one student you saw today at school do better at something or feel better about something, who would it be and what would you do to help them?" "What's one thing your teacher does that really helps you learn better?" "What's one thing you don't look forward to at recess?"

We'd just keep passing the tennis ball back and forth. I learned to listen and they learned how to begin sharing their heart.

Again, don't get discouraged by short answers or rolling eyes. Keep asking questions and taking mental notes on the answers you're given. Remember, this is an intentional conversation in which you are striving to connect with your son or daughter and express to them that they matter to you.

It's also fun to do with a neighbor child or other friend who's in the car with your kids. In other words, you announce, "OK, we're playing 20 Questions as we take you home." Then you start by handing your child the ball first and their answering a question; then you hand their friend the ball and they have to answer a question. You can't imagine how many times one of our kids' friends got in the car and wanted to play 20 Questions! I think in part because they hadn't had anyone else take an interest in what they were thinking or saying—they hadn't been made to feel that what they had to say was valuable to hear!

I've mentioned riding in the car. You can also do this on a bike ride with an active child. When you take a break, you can say, "OK, while we rest, we're going to play 20 Questions." Then ask your question and toss them the ball.

It's a small thing—passing a tennis ball back and forth—but it's one great way to build those spoken-word lines of communication.

Becoming-the-Family-IT-Servant-and-Taking-Your-Family-Off-the-Grid Blessing

With my challenge for you to play 20 Questions with your child with a tennis ball, you may have been wondering, *Is there an app for that to come up with questions?* If you thought that, it's because most parents today have grown up with technology. Maybe you're old enough to remember that ear-piercing dial-up sound, but if you're like most parents today, you've probably had the latest-and-greatest high-speed technology since the time you first started school.

And because you know so much about technology and if you're serious about being a father who blesses his son or daughter, then you know there's an equal but opposite error many parents make. Either they demand that there be no technology in their home (and then they watch their child's teacher scream and their child wail that they can't do their homework or get their assignment from their teacher without the Internet!) or they just give in and don't bother monitoring what their child does online. Actually, *don't* do that. Ignoring your child's use of technology today is almost a guarantee you'll see him or her spending more and more time in front of a screen and then seeing that screen devour their real-life relationship with you and others—and even their Lord. So what's a father to do?

Here are two ways to bless your child in regard to technology. First, *lean into technology—even if it's a challenge for you.* I know you're busy. But you need to know what's going on with technology today, because there are so many ways it can eat away at your relationship with your child if you don't. So start out by reading some good books on the wise use of technology, like Gary Chapman and Arlene

Pellicane's book *Growing Up Social.* Set boundaries. Don't operate out of fear, but be aware that there are terrible people a child can meet and horrible places a child can go by using technology. Use filters, and do your best to stay involved with what your children are doing and seeing and playing. Be the family Apple genius in your home!

Because you're going to have technology in your home, *you* need to be the one who deals with computer issues or problems. Of course you might not be a real Apple genius (who can solve in seconds what you've struggled with for hours). But whether you're a PC person or Mac person, *you* be the one who knows how to connect the printer to the computer. Whatever the operating system is in your home, *you* be the one who knows how to get things connected, upgraded, and rebooted. If the printer stops printing, have extra ink cartridges on hand for those late-night papers (which caused the old ones to run out). Make a business card with "IT Family Servant" on it, and give it to your kids. And make sure they know that you'll do your best to be the head of the home IT department. This doesn't mean you have to know every program. Nor is your goal to join every social media site and try to be their friend on everything. But the more you know, the better you can step in to help them in a tech crisis—and the more you'll know about what they're doing online and with technology and if there's a problem with what they see or where they go. So being the IT servant in your home is one way you can bless, or add to, the life of your child and your family. But there's something I think is even more important.

Second, while leaning into technology, *be the one in your family who leads everyone off the grid one hour each week!* We started doing that in our home—and it was an amazing experience. Every Wednesday night came to be called Off-the-Grid Night. Meaning, the kids could use technology from the time they got home to get their homework done, but after dinner, everything "went dark." We went off the grid and back in time to a place where, for an hour or two, nothing that runs on batteries or plugs into the wall could be used in the home. (Refrigerator and heater or air conditioner were of course excluded.)

To begin that time, I'd yell, "The grid's down!" and our kids would come running into the living room. When they came into the room, there would be something there for us all to do. I'd have a big piece of butcher paper on the table and crayons or markers and a task for us to draw a family mural. We'd actually play a family board game. (There are so many good ones!) We'd have a book for each child and adult. We'd spend some time reading alone and then share with the family one thing we enjoyed from our reading. We'd do an anything-goes dinner: we'd drive to the store and each family member could pick one thing for dinner, and we'd come home and make it. (And yes, there were times when we had more than one dessert as a main course). One of the best off-the-grid activities involved setting a pretty big cardboard box in the middle of the room, and for an hour, the kids had to just come up with things to do with the cardboard box. That box became a fort, something we took outside and slid down a hill on, a hammock (with people being tossed onto pillows), etc.

You bless children when you relate to them. So by being the family IT servant, you get to step in and be the one in charge of fixing or updating computers and printers (And at the same time, see what's happening in your family tech wise.) But you also get to be the one who leads the way in getting them to unplug at times and spend time as a family relating to each other. Spending time with you—that's a blessing.

— 3 —

Pack-Rat Blessing

 Detailed organization is not my strong suit. Those of you who keep your email inbox empty would cringe, maybe even panic, if you opened my email account. If you are a person who can't stand clutter and continually feels the urge to throw things away, then this suggestion of how to bless your son or daughter may be a little (or a lot) outside of your comfort zone. But I would challenge you to become a positive pack-rat in this regard.

In short, look for things you can keep and put away in a "treasure box"—things that to your child represent what was at the time an important event, experience, or feeling in their life story. Maybe not earth shattering in the grand scheme of things—but huge to them. And to bless them, make it important to you as well.

Like the program from their first piano recital. Or the church program that just reads "Child Dedication"—but it was *your* child being dedicated. Ask the coach of your child's team if you could have the scorecard after the game or the lineup card from that game. Your treasures might include a piece of art they created or that note they wrote you or even a letter to Santa that you found (even though they now know that Santa isn't real). Each is a small thing but a big deal down the road when you pull it out of the box.

I realize that you may bemoan the thought of all these pictures and tokens and things taking up space. But imagine the value that these small things can have when you pull them out years later. That third-place ribbon from field day. That ticket from their first circus or that movie that you all liked so well.

I'm not asking you to be super organized or to make a scrapbook or a shadowbox to show off all these memorable items. Just throw them in a designated box that you'll get to one day. And on that day when your children are much older—which will come incredibly soon—it's amazing how those little things you saved can bring back so many memories of positive times. *And* memories of tough times (when they forgot their piece at the recital or blew the game with an error). But each treasure will say, "I was there with you. You rocked." Even if they didn't win the game. You'll be amazed at the words and ways you can bless them when you go down memory lane—and the ways they've blessed your life as well.

4

Late-Night Blessing

 As your children get older (and so do you!), there will soon come a time when they are staying up later than you do. While you may have fond memories of your children falling asleep in their car seats on the way home and your delicately transferring them into their beds, things will change before you know it. Instead, your son will be waking you up, saying, "Dad, you fell

asleep watching the movie again." Don't miss the opportunity to bless your son or daughter—even in your sleep.

My twin brother and I often went on double dates in high school. I'm not sure how we started the tradition, but when we got home, Jeff and I would wake Mom up to talk about our dates or whatever else was on our minds.

I remember once asking her, "Mom, does it bother you that we wake you up to talk?"

I will never forget her response, and I've used the same words with my own daughters:

> "John, wake me up anytime. I can always go back to sleep, but I won't always have you boys around to talk to."

Do you hear the elements of the blessing laced into those words? What a powerful way to show your incredible love to your son or daughter. We're so scheduled so much of the time—we're so busy. But what if your child knew that even if they woke you up, you'd be ready (even though you might take time to brew a quick cup of coffee) to talk with them, to listen to them.

Trust me, they won't ask you every night. You'll get plenty of sleep in the aggregate over time. But let them know that if they need you, you're ready to talk. "I can always go back to sleep, but I won't always have you around to talk to."

They may be ready to talk to you when you're in the car or on the way to the mall or just before bed. And yes, they might want to talk when it's the fourth quarter of the game (which is why you choose to use the DVR and save each game, even as you start watching it).

But being ready to listen to their joys, sorrows, fears, and dreams whenever they are ready to talk will strengthen your relationship beyond measure and bless them richly. The turbulent teen years can be ones of strained communication, but if you choose to be available to your son or daughter when they want to talk, you may find that they are much more willing to share about what is truly going on in their mind, heart, and life.

5

Cool-Kid Blessing

I have no doubt that your son or daughter is different from what you anticipated before they were born. However, I would challenge you to choose to bless your child by looking for ways in which they have *exceeded your expectations*. Maybe they are kinder than you imagined they would be, more generous, more academic, or more athletic.

My daughter Kari was the head cheerleader for the varsity squad during her senior year. Admirably, the whole squad voted to include a girl with cerebral palsy as a squad member for the year. I cannot tell you how my heart swelled with pride as I watched Kari include this awesome young lady who was confined to a wheelchair. Kari would stand by her, pick up her pom-poms when she dropped them, get her a drink of water (it's hot in Arizona, even at night), and make sure she got into the huddle with the other girls. I remember telling her after watching her so obviously love on her friend Brooke, "Kari, do you know that you are even neater than the daughter that we prayed for? I was an athlete in high school and college. I saw a lot of cheerleaders. But I never saw one who showed others more love and compassion than you've shown Brooke this year."

Yes, there are times when that same child is going to frustrate you. When they'll do something that's selfish or inconsiderate. But don't look for perfection before you bless a son or daughter. When God opens your eyes and you see it, let them know that they've exceeded your expectations. Like Kari did in helping her friend Brooke. Proverbs 3:27 (ESV) says, "Do not withhold good from those to whom it is due, when it is in your power to do it." It's in your power to bless your children, and one way to do that is to point out to them a trait or something positive they're doing that's just amazing to you—perhaps even more amazing than what you prayed for before their arrival!

6

Secret-Handshake Blessing

 While meaningful touch can and should be interwoven into many of the other ways I have mentioned of passing on the blessing, I want to make sure I encourage you to make a habit of looking for ways and times in which you can bless your son or daughter without a word being spoken. That's the incredibly powerful way that appropriate meaningful touch can bless your son or daughter.

This aspect of the blessing—appropriate meaningful touch—was something I had to really work on. I grew up in Arizona where it's OK to hug your horse, not your kids. On top of that, I grew up with a mother who was a rheumatoid arthritic, so she couldn't hug you; if she did, it hurt her joints so much she'd cry. She was also gone for months at a time, hospitalized. Because of all her surgeries and arthritis, my mom never remarried, so I didn't grow up touching or hugging or seeing it as part of what a family does. And I also grew up angry. I pushed people away until I was in high school. I didn't want them coming close. But after I became a Christian, God blew a hole in that side of myself. In large part, that was because of what I saw in Doug Barram, the man I mentioned earlier who led me to Christ.

If you'll remember, Doug was a big (six foot four) offensive tackle in college. And he was a hugger—something I hated at the time. He would show up at our football practices and high-five, put out a huge hand for a handshake, and even (cringe) put his arm around your shoulder, if it was appropriate. I had never had a grown man reach out to me. Yet there was Doug, modeling appropriate meaningful touch. That handshake when he met you. His arm around me when we lost a big playoff game my senior year in football. His bear hug when I won a championship in wrestling and got mobbed after the match.

I watched Doug bless his wife and his children with so many small acts of meaningful touch. For example, if you ate dinner at Doug's house (which a bunch of us football guys did each week), you had to hold hands around the table when you prayed over the food. And before you dropped the hand of the person sitting next to you after the prayer, you had to squeeze the guy's hand four times, which meant "I love you, Joe " (or whatever the name was of the person whose hand you held). After dinner, he'd get all us football guys to walk down the hall with his two young boys and help him put them to bed. Doug would stand there in the hallway. He'd pick up the oldest boy first, pray a blessing over him, and then toss him across the room into bed. Then he'd do the same for the younger one. I'll be honest: it seemed so natural to him and so unnatural to me. Yet it was those small acts of appropriate meaningful touch with his family that really sold me on becoming a Christian like him! My dad left our family when I was two months old. I never held his hand until the day he was dying. I cannot tell you how much seeing a grown, godly man love and bless and appropriately touch his kids impacted my life. And how much it has helped me bless my children.

Which is why I started working on being a hugger. And over time, it worked. Now I hold my wife's hand at the mall, instead of just walking ahead of her. I hug my girls when I walk in the door and before they head to bed.

I know some families who have come up with their own secret handshake to use with their son or daughter—a secret handshake to greet them when they come home from school or hop in the car after band practice or to celebrate a goal they scored on the soccer field.

I don't get to see Doug Barram very often anymore. But I know one thing. When I do get to see him, even though decades have passed since we were young, I'm going to get a hug from him. And because of him, my children are going to look back at me and say, "Dad didn't leave out that part of the blessing." Touch was such an important part of how Jesus interacted with people—not just hurting people but even children: "He took the children in his arms, placed his hands on them and blessed them" (Mark 10:16, NIV). So even if you're like me and touch wasn't there when you were young—or if you were only "touched" in anger—look for those creative ways (like a secret handshake) and consistent ways (like holding their hand and praying for them at night before bed) when your appropriate meaningful touch can say, without words, that your child has your blessing.

7

Kodak-Moment Blessing

While I appreciate my iPhone and the advances in technology I am privileged to use on a daily basis, I will say, I'm grateful that in my young adult years, Facebook and Instagram weren't around yet. When our wedding was approaching, I had a serious lapse in judgment about what I would wear on our wedding day. Lured by a deeply discounted price, I purchased light gray, extra-wide lapel, double-breasted tuxes with bell-bottom pants for myself and my groomsmen. Oh, how I would regret that decision years later when my daughters discovered our wedding photos. I can't imagine what it would be like if the images were posted all over the Internet like they instantly could be these days. How embarrassing. When Kari was in kindergarten or first grade, she noticed the lovely white wedding album high on the shelf and asked if she could look at the pictures. She saw me for the first time with big hair, a bushy mustache, and overgrown sideburns; and her belly laughing could not be contained. After that, the girls wanted to pull down the album every time they had a friend over. Eventually, I conceded to a tradition of looking at the photos every year on our anniversary.

Have you ever taken the opportunity to show your child pictures from your life before they were born? Whether you've gained weight, lost hair, or improved your style, swallow your pride and pull out your old photos to share with your children. Or, perhaps even better, if you have them, break out old home videos and make some popcorn for a good time of laughter. Children love to see images of their parents when they were young, and connecting to their heritage has value far beyond the blush that may come to your cheeks. You are an example to your son or daughter of how God can use someone's life in powerful ways. Seeing images of your past and being acquainted with your present gives them a real life story to attach to and see that God uses all sorts of people in all sorts of ways. As you look at old photos or watch old videos with your kids, talk to them about how God encouraged you or taught you things at various points in your life. Ask your son or daughter what they are learning right now about God and about people. Imagine with them what the photos in their albums might look like in the future. As you reflect on old memories, create new memories with your son or daughter, and picture a special future with them.

8

Backyard-and-Family-Camp Blessing

 My wife, Cindy, grew up camping. I grew up in a single-parent home with a mom with rheumatoid arthritis, so camping was out of the question. But Cindy and I had kids. And one day a friend pulled into our driveway with a huge RV, and a powerful way to bless our children happened.

You have a friend like this particular friend, I'm sure. You know the guy who as a kid couldn't wait to ride his supercool BMX bike over on Christmas morning, when the coolest thing you got was socks. That's the guy who showed up in my driveway, blaring the horn on his new, ginormous RV, complete with a back bedroom, huge kitchen and dining area, bathroom, and television. And yes, he and his family were heading out to go camping. But he just wanted to show me what he had bought before he headed out with his kids and wife for a great weekend in the pine trees.

That did it. I was a youth pastor, not making great money of course, but I wasn't going to let that stop me from going camping. I drove over to the local big-box store, found the camping aisle, and got a tent, a lantern (yes, one of the old-style ones that were impossible to light), and a camp stove (made by the same people who make the lantern impossible to light).

I got home and announced, "We're going camping!" The kids went crazy. Only slightly less so when I explained to them, "We're going backyard camping." And that's what we did. We started out with putting up the tent—without directions of course, which would have been a sign of weakness. Then we started to cook dinner on our camp stove, which never lit, so Cindy had to cook everything inside. And then for light, there was that lantern—the one that would in a flash burn to cinders those little nets—and the flashlights—the ones that would have worked had I remembered to get batteries ahead of time. In short, by morning, while we started out as a whole family in the tent, at dawn there was just me and one of our two dogs, the one who can sleep through earthquakes. And that's when the sprinklers went on.

So began a great in-town adventure. Several times each year, I'd announce we were going camping. And I'd listen to the groans and drag out and dust off all the camping equipment. But we got better. Not at the lantern or stove, which we sold at a garage sale. But at coming up with camp games and even a way to make a fire for s'mores (we used an old barbecue).

In lots of things in life, chaos and failure aren't good things. Amazingly, when it comes to family times, it's when things go wrong—and our first attempt at camping defines things going wrong—that amazing memories are produced and children feel loved and blessed (after the mosquito bites and upset stomachs from late-night junk food pass).

Not sold on backyard camping? Then go to a real

campground. Or rent an RV for a weekend. Or do what we'd do to bless our children: we started going to a Christian family camp one weekend during the school year and, later as the kids got older, one week during the summer. There are so many great camps—literally hundreds of them—that do outstanding family camps (just go to www.cciworldwide.org, and you can find one near you). Typically during the day, parents and kids enjoy age-graded programs and then join together for fun activities in the afternoon and evening. There are often a variety of things like zip-lining, horseback riding, archery, crafts, games, outdoor water sports, and more for an incredibly reasonable price. There may even be scholarships available for families. Or perhaps your church does a family weekend or camping experience that you can participate in. Or do what we did and do a backyard campout. It's a great way to connect with each person in your family and enjoy God's creation (particularly if you remember to turn off the sprinklers), and it's a time that is guaranteed to bless your son or daughter as they look back on all that happened.

9

Saltshaker Blessings

 I grew up with two brothers, and inevitably, we got in fights on a regular basis. But I can still hear my mother's voice saying at least a hundred times, "That's your brother. Don't hit him." Or, "You only have two brothers. You don't hit your brother." My mom did an excellent job of teaching us that brother relationships are important—special. To this day, my brothers and I are close. Not being given free rein to beat up on each other emotionally or physically, we bonded in a positive way.

I've strived to do the same thing with my daughters. Challenging them to cherish each other as sisters, even when there is drama, has proven so valuable. Kari and Laura have drastically different personalities. You'll learn more about using each person's personality strengths in a later section, but here, I want you to focus on building a positive relationship between your children. Because we continually stressed the importance of the sister relationship, Kari and Laura share a love and commitment to each other and to our family that we are very proud of and thankful for.

In part, that love and commitment happened because we took time as a family to pass the saltshaker of honor. Here's what I mean by that and how it can help you bless your children.

We have one daughter who loves to talk. Cindy, my wife, and I both are loud and verbal. And we have another daughter who sees everything and is a great listener but may not always feel like trying to fight her way into the conversation. It was noticing that Laura wasn't talking at meals that made me ask her, "What's wrong, honey? Why aren't you talking?"

"It's OK, Dad," she said. "I don't have to talk. You guys do all the talking for me." The way she said that revealed that she wasn't angry. It actually reflected sadness. Or perhaps just a resignation that she wasn't one of the loud ones, so she kept quiet at the table.

That led to the saltshaker of honor showing up at the table the next night.

"Here's what we're going to do," I announced. "This isn't just any saltshaker. This is the saltshaker of honor. Meaning, each of us is going to get a turn to talk as we hold the saltshaker of honor. No one else can interrupt or break in. When that person is done talking, then you pass the saltshaker of honor to the person to your right, and we're going to go all the way around the table, with each person getting a chance to talk and everyone else listening."

It didn't go great the first night. But the saltshaker of honor—where we sought to really honor each person by listening and valuing them—showed up the next night. And the next. And amazingly, we really did, at least while the saltshaker was present, start listening. And we discovered that Laura really did have a voice.

Passing the saltshaker is still a great family game we play when we're all around the table now and there's so much to catch up on. Each person gets a chance to talk, and we honor one another by really listening—a small way to bless your children . . . and spouse!

10

Protective-Pop Blessing

While I didn't witness it, I've been told that Cindy's grandfather would tease her and her brothers past the limit. I've heard that he would take a toy from a child and not give it back until tears of frustration were shed. While I never saw Cindy being teased in this way, I did see her father teasing our daughter by doing things very similar to what his father had done with him and his children.

I had a wonderful relationship with Cindy's parents before they passed away, and I was much closer to Cindy's father than I was to my own. But when I saw my father-in-law excessively teasing Kari, I put my foot down.

I asked my father-in-law to step outside, and I spoke with him privately and told him how much I loved, appreciated, and valued him; how much I loved his daughter; and how we loved having him be a part of our family and hanging out with the girls when they were in town. But I also told him a story:

"Remember when you were back in Wisconsin on the dairy farm?"

"Absolutely," he said.

"Remember how you told me how much trouble you and your friend got into as a kid when you kept chasing some of the cows and they got scared and quit giving milk?"

He completely remembered that story he had told me from his childhood.

"I couldn't sit down for a week after that!" he said, and it may not have been an exaggeration, from what I know about his father.

"So guess what, Dad. You're scaring the cows into not giving any milk."

There was a long pause.

"I don't get it," he said.

"I know that it was OK in your family for your father to tease the kids and grandkids until they got so frustrated, they cried. Cindy told me about that. And I see you doing that with our kids. But I want you to know that it doesn't help them when you do that. It hurts them. It makes them stop wanting to be around you, not want to step towards you. So from now on, teasing the kids at our house is like chasing the cows. It needs to stop."

There was another long pause, and my father-in-law nodded his head.

And I literally never had to talk to him about it again.

Now keep something in mind. In the book of Proverbs, it says, "Do not rebuke mockers or they will hate you; rebuke the wise and they will love you" (Proverbs 9:8, NIV). I realize that stepping in to protect a child or lovingly trying to confront a wrong past family pattern can cause the person you're confronting hurt—particularly if you're confronting someone who is immature or foolish. But Cindy's dad was an old bomber pilot from World War II.

A builder. At the end of his life, he even became a believer. In short, he was a man of honor, and, to his credit, he got the picture and stopped doing what he could now see was causing his grandchildren to step away from him, not towards him.

Yet a big reason why he got the picture was because I used a picture to confront him! Such a picture is called an emotional word picture, and using one is a great way to link a picture to the thing you want to share with someone. It helps them really see what they're doing in a way that words sometimes can't describe.

A great way to bless your children then is to step in and protect them—from a teacher who's said something way over the line, a coach who's done something that's wrong, a grandparent who's trying to be funny or loving but not coming across that way to a child. Jesus talks about how those who would cause a little one to stumble are in serious trouble (Matthew 18: 6-7; Luke 17:1-3). So it's important to step in when it's appropriate to do so. And when you do, look for that word picture that can, in a positive way, help them see what they're doing. (Need help in coming up with word pictures? Look for *The Language of Love*, the book all about word pictures that Gary Smalley and I wrote. Also read 2 Samuel 12:1–7. It's the story of how Nathan went before David, the king, and confronted him with a story. And it changed the king's life.)

If you have a good relationship with your parents, other relatives, and/or in-laws, and you deem any of their behavior around your child inappropriate, stand up for your son or daughter. You have the responsibility to protect your children and stand in the battle for them. I hope that when the situation is explained with sensitivity and respect, your relationship with the person will be strengthened rather than threatened. Sometimes, the outcome is not as rosy as that of my encounter with my father-in-law, such as what happened when my own father stormed away angrily when I told him that he was welcome in our home but not if he'd been drinking. You show your children that they are valuable when you protect them and seek to create an environment of safety and security for them. Be strong and courageous. Your children are worth it.

11

Spiritual-"Toothpaste" Blessing

One of the greatest ways you can bless your son or daughter is by stepping up to bring faith home to your children. Right there, I know I'm going to lose you if you're like me and never saw what a spiritual leader looks like up close and personal. But don't bail out on this way to bless your children until you answer this question: Can you squeeze a toothpaste tube?

Because if you can, you've got the makings of someone who can absolutely bring faith home to your family! Here's what I mean.

As I mentioned earlier, we didn't do family devotions or family altars or family anything really in my home growing up. My mother was a wonderful person, but we just didn't know much about Jesus or faith in him. We certainly didn't talk about him at home. If Jesus' name was spoken, it usually resulted in someone's mouth being washed out with soap, not in everyone's faith being strengthened. Even after I came to Christ, I didn't have a clear picture of what it looked like to "train up a child in the way he should go" (Proverbs 22:6, ESV). But when Cindy and I did have children, we talked, and then we set out to bless our children with the greatest gift we could give them: coming to know Jesus as their own personal Lord and Savior—and knowing how to build a relationship with him and walk well with others like he did!

So that started Family Nights for us. And each Family Night would always begin with me putting on loud music and a song that the kids loved to dance to. I'd yell out, "It's Family Night time!" and then hit the play button. On would come a Beach Boys song or something else great to dance to. Cindy and the girls would pile out of their rooms, run down the hall, and immediately break into dance in the family room. They all love to dance for some reason. They all also loved begging me to stop dancing when I joined then.

Next, I'd turn off the music and I'd always start with a question like, "OK, kids! Here's tonight's question for Family Night: Is it harder to do something or undo something?" Not waiting for an answer, I'd have them head over to our old kitchen table.

At the table, we had four toothpaste tubes, one for each person in our family. (This is an example of just how simple yet incredibly positive and helpful even doing something like squeezing a toothpaste tube can be in passing down your faith in Jesus to your children!)

I told them that we were going to have a family contest. I explained to them that everyone was going to get a paper plate and a brand-new toothpaste tube, and I would put on the table a crisp, new dollar bill. Everyone was told, "The first one to squeeze out onto the paper plate in front of them all the toothpaste from their tube will win the $1.00 bill." Then I'd say, "Ready, set, go!" and Cindy and I would let one of the kids win. Imagine doing that with your family. It's really fun watching everyone's efforts to squeeze all of the gooey paste out of the tubes.

If you want to head off fights, you can always declare a tie and give each child a dollar. But whoever wins, keep an eye on your watch and say, "That was only thirty seconds! Great job!" And then talk about how easy or hard it was to do something—like squeezing out toothpaste from a tube.

Then tell them that there will be a second contest, and take out a $20 bill! If they're anything like our kids, watch their eyes light up when they see the $20! Tell them, "OK, here we go. The person in the family who is able to get back into their tube *all* the toothpaste on their plate, wins this $20 bill!"

Now you may be thinking, *They're too smart for that*. And your wife may be thinking the same thing. But just watch the kids. They'll push and shove, and finally someone will take some of the toothpaste and really try to complete the task. In our home, it was Laura who attempted to put a bunch of the toothpaste in her mouth and spit it back into the tube. Which made for a fantastic foaming-at-the-mouth family photo.

Once all members have given up (and they will—eventually), spend a few minutes cleaning up and gather back together in the living room. Open your Bible up to Psalm 15 and read verse 3: "[The righteous person] does not slander with his tongue" (ESV).

Explain that what they just did with the toothpaste is an example of why we must take care not to hurt people with our words. Tell them, "When you say something wrong or bad or mean to someone, it's like squeezing out all the toothpaste from the tube. And it is pretty easy to say something. But once your words come out, it's really hard—often impossible—to get them back. That's why God wants us to be careful not to say hurtful words. They can stay in people's memories and hearts a long, long time." After you've made your point, pray with your family and ask God to give each of you wisdom in the words that you speak to and about others.

We'd then have a dessert that Cindy had made. In just that short amount of time, we had fun, learned something from God's Word, and learned something about living like Jesus—all based on our just having them squeeze a toothpaste tube.

Which is why if you can blow up a balloon or squeeze a toothpaste tube or do one of a hundred other things like that, you can teach a spiritual principle to your son or daughter. You don't have to have been to seminary or have ever seen a spiritual leader in your home. You get to be one in your family. And it's moments like that with your son or daughter and wife that matter so much in passing down your faith to your child, in giving them that incredible blessing of learning to love God and his life-changing Word as a part of your home culture.

12

Prayer-Standard-Time Blessing

 Similar to how we ask "How are you?" on autopilot, without even paying attention to the answer, I can't even tell you how often I've been guilty of saying "I'll pray for you" when someone has shared something with me and then I've forgotten to follow through. If you're like me, you don't forget out of malicious intent, by any means. We usually really want to pray for the person. We just get busy or other concerns of life step in the way of our intention. Then we end up at the end of the day without having ever prayed for that need or person.

It was that realization of prayers un-prayed—and a new watch—that gave me another way to bless my children.

It was Christmas and I had gotten just what I had been wanting: a new really cool sport watch with not one but three timers and two alarm clocks! Meaning I was thinking of all the things I could time using my cool new watch. Even though school was out, Kari, our oldest, had volleyball practice coming up. This meant lots of hard work, even though all her other friends were hanging out and resting up on vacation.

"Pray for my practice tomorrow." She said. And of course I said, "I will." And then I stopped and said, "So, Kari, what time is your practice tomorrow?"

"It's at 2 p.m.," she said. And I had something I could set on the second alarm clock on my wrist. The next day came and, sure enough, at 2 p.m. my watch's alarm went off. And I was totally confused. I could not for the world remember why the alarm had been set for 2 p.m. Then it dawned on me: Kari's practice.

And from that time on, whenever someone— particularly my kids—asked me to pray for them or had a big test or an upcoming interview or project due, I'd set my watch to Prayer Standard Time. And I can't even tell you how often that alarm would go off, and I'd initially be at a total loss as to why. And then I'd remember why I set the alarm, and then I'd remember to bless my child (or sometimes another person) by remembering to pray for them.

Perhaps you are someone who lives by your daily planner or your smartphone calendar or even your email inbox. Try setting up a calendar event to pray for your son or daughter. Write it on your checklist in your planner. Use whatever works for you to set up a system to remind yourself to pray for your son or daughter; and when you get the reminder, pray! As a bonus, write out a prayer for your son or daughter, or send your child an email or text message letting them know that you are praying for them.

A Scripture Blessing

 While God's Word doesn't need any words added or taken away from it, I think that God is honored when we use Scripture to speak blessing over our children. There are tons of Scriptures that you can use to speak a

blessing over your son or daughter. You might make a big deal about speaking a Scripture over your son or daughter as part of celebrating their birthday. Birthdays are a great time to give both a spoken and written blessing to your son or daughter—a way of commemorating the occasion of reaching a new age. You can paraphrase Scripture to apply more specifically to your son or daughter while still communicating the truths of God's words. Make it a personal experience. Let me give you a couple of examples. If your son's name is Jim, you might say a blessing like this for him:

> "Jim, I pray that you will listen to what
> the Lord says and treasure his commands.
> I hope that you will open up your ears to
> wisdom and concentrate on understanding.
> I pray, Jim, that you will ask tough questions
> and search for answers.
> Search for them as you would for silver;
> seek them like hidden treasures."
>
> [Proverbs 2:1-4]

If your daughter's name is Ashley, you might write a blessing like this for her:

> *"Ashley, I know that you want*
> *to be close to God.*
> *I pray you will obey him*
> *and do what is right.*
> *Ashley, I pray that you will speak the truth*
> *and never spread gossip.*
> *Treat others fairly*
> *and keep from saying mean things.*
> *Don't bother with people*
> *who don't want to do what is right,*
> *but listen to those who love*
> *and worship God."*
>
> [Psalm 15:1-4]

Some other great Scriptures that may help you get started are Psalm 1; Proverbs 1:1-7; 3:1-6; 4:23-25. Speaking the truths of God's Word over your son or daughter is a great way to bless them.

Pick-a-Holiday-to-Help-Others Blessing

 Holidays are often a time when kids can get very focused on gaining things for themselves. However, I challenge you to guide your children to choose a holiday to make a special effort to give to others. You can choose whether to give money or time and talent, but make a plan to sacrifice together for the benefit of someone else. As a family, make a trip to a local shelter to help feed the homeless a meal. Or spend a number of weeks collecting change together to give to a charity. Spend some time praying for those who you will impact and talk about how it feels to give to others. Choose to spend a holiday blessing your kids by getting them out of their comfort zone and challenging them to be a part of blessing others as well.

Tipping-Service Blessing

 I have a great memory of a time my mother took my two brothers and I out to eat when my twin and I were ten years old and my older brother was twelve. Because I lived in a single-parent household, going out to eat wasn't something that we did regularly, and it was always treated as a special occasion. But I remember this time even more vividly than any other. My mother had decided that it was time for us to demonstrate some additional responsibility, so, at dinner, she announced to us that she would no longer be the one paying the bill when we went out to eat.

While she wasn't expecting us to come up with the money to pay the bill, she wanted us to learn the practice of tipping our server. She talked with us about the concept of tipping with regard to the quality of service that was rendered. We had learned in math how to calculate percentages, so we talked about giving a smaller percentage for adequate service and a larger percentage for exceptional service (or 0 percent for absolutely terrible service and discussing the incident with the manager). From then on, my brothers and I handled calculating the tip and, with money from our mother, going through the process of paying the bill.

The experience of learning to pay the bill helped both my brothers and I learn more about what it costs to eat out and what quality service really looks like. We learned to pay attention to the details of service in a way that we never had before. I chose to continue this learning experience with my girls when they reached an appropriate age. It's a small thing, but it's a way to help your children see how much eating out really costs and how they can bless, or encourage, someone with a tip that says "Job well done." Christians are sometimes believed to be poor tippers. (I worked as a waiter for seven years during college and graduate school, and I can personally attest to too many tracts being left instead of tips; and I remember other waiters grumbling, "I saw my people pray. There goes my tip.") You don't have to over-tip poor service, but talk about being generous as a way of blessing others who are working hard to serve you.

— 16 —
Sponsor-Your-Kid Blessing

 I once counseled a couple in the middle of a heartbreaking and messy divorce. They were parents to three children under ten years old, two of them girls. The mother had thrown the father out, not as a result of drugs, sex, or alcohol, but because of the way he selfishly handled the family's money. With his wife and children, the man held very tightly to the purse strings. He would deem as frivolous and refuse to pay for what could have been meaningful experiences that the children wanted to participate in. When his daughters wanted to join a gymnastics class, he labeled the cost as prohibitive and responded with a firm no to their request. When it came to his own interests, however, the man was extravagant in his spending. The same week he

denied his daughters the experience of gymnastics, he purchased one new golf club for more than $450. He rationalized his behavior as being "for business purposes." The mother had finally reached her limit when he denied her funds to take her daughter to a Christmas card-making party at $15 per person (including a catered meal!) but within a week chose to spend $3,000 on an extravagant golfing trip. Again he defended himself saying, "But that was business."

Business wasn't really what that father was thinking about, however. He was thinking about himself. His choices to continually deny his family meaningful experiences wasn't to protect them financially; it was to hoard the family's financial resources for his own benefit. Sadly, many fathers fail to see the value of paying for music lessons when their daughter will never be a first-chair violinist, paying for gymnastics when their child will never be an Olympian, or paying for a mother to take her daughter to make memories as well as cards when the cards will just get thrown away later. Today, that dad is paying for his choices in the form of child support and alimony.

Choosing to invest in your children's (and your

wife's) interests may cost you some money, but the benefits of your family feeling loved and valued will be beyond measure.

17

Go-Cart Blessing

I will never forget that after enjoying the Disneyland autobahn ride on a family trip, Kari, who had steered the slow-moving car, announced, "I'm ready to get my driver's license!" She was only seven or eight, but that didn't quench her enthusiasm. I encouraged her that she would be an excellent driver someday, though that wasn't the day!

That day did come all too soon, but in the meantime, I made it a priority to give my daughters opportunities to drive long before they made the trip to the driver's-license office to get their learner's permits. Don't worry. I'm not advocating sticking your child behind the steering wheel of your car on the open road (or even a back road!), but there are plenty of ways that kids can get opportunities to drive early on. Hit up the family go-cart tracks, or let your older child steer the boat when you are way in the middle of the lake without other boats around (and stay within close reach of that wheel!). Take note of the way that your child drives in these environments, and give encouragement and direction. Start teaching the basics of safe driving early. Make the most of those moments to talk about the great responsibility of driving, and challenge your kids to take it very seriously. When Kari finally got her driver's permit, she was more confident than most of her friends, and I continued to give her as many opportunities to practice as I could before she passed the exam and was able to cruise the streets solo.

18

Dad-Taxicab Blessing

I would encourage you to man the taxicab in your son or daughter's life. Before you know it, they'll be driving themselves, and your opportunities to connect during car time will be severely limited. Make the most of the time you have with them now by being the one carting them from place to place. Offer to pick up friends, take them to the show they want to see, or be the one who is there when practice lets out. Your child's preteen years are the time when there is a great need for this in your son or daughter's life. You may be resistant to the idea of being the taxi driver, but it is an incredible way to bless your child. Show them that their activities and friends are just as important as yours and that you are committed to being the transportation.

19

iPod Blessing

 My daughters have demonstrated an incredible variety of musical taste over the years. From Veggie Tales to pop, many a tune has been heard in our house. As our girls grew, we monitored what music they listened to personally, but I also always made it a point to stock my car with some of their favorite stuff to jam out to. Music plays a powerful role in the lives of children and is a great way to connect with your son or daughter. When my girls were young, my car had a six-CD changer, and since I basically listen exclusively to talk radio, I gave my daughters the freedom to stock all six slots with their favorites. I would take them to the mall and let them each choose two CDs that were exclusively for listening to in my car. After several months, they could add the CDs to their collection and get some new ones to fill the slots. It gave me the opportunity to hear what they enjoyed

and resonated with and to connect with them on a different level.

Maybe you have an iPod or your phone automatically syncs with your car stereo. Every few months, take some time to let your son or daughter create their own playlists for your car. When they ride with you, listen to their music and ask them questions about the artists, their favorite songs, why they like a particular style of music, etc. The blessing is all about expressing genuine love and unconditional acceptance. Often music is something that kids and parents have very different taste in, but if you make a special effort to demonstrate interest in your son or daughter's music, there may be fewer battles in your home about who gets to control the stereo.

⟨20⟩

Literary-Hero Blessing

 At some point during the wonder-filled days of childhood, make a point to read through *The Chronicles of Narnia* by C. S. Lewis with your son or daughter. These books make great read-aloud bedtime stories that can take weeks to complete. As a bonus, though, let your son or daughter star as one of the great characters in the series. Make sure to choose one of the characters that remain faithful throughout the tales. Lucy is a great choice for girls and Peter is a great choice for boys. As you read, simply replace the character's name with your son or daughter's name. Your child will have the added excitement of imagining themselves as a hero or heroine. Plus, the experience will expose your child to one of history's most renowned thinkers and theologians.

21

Friendship Blessing

Something we probably all want for our children is for them to have lasting friendships. Who doesn't want great friends that stick with you through thick and thin? While our need for acceptance within our family is certainly crucial, we have a desire for lasting relationships outside of our family as well.

One of the things that was difficult to watch my girls go through was each of them being confronted with the truth that not all friends are friends for life. Fortunately, I sought to protect them in advance by having a conversation with them about disappearing friends. With each daughter, I shared with them the biblical account of Christ's betrayal by Judas in the Upper Room. Before we faced the hurt of a disappearing friend in each of their lives, I shared the story and asked them what they thought Jesus felt when Judas betrayed him. The discussion then led me to ask, "Have you ever had a friend who you really liked, and they walked away from you or hurt you by something they did or said?" I was surprised that each of them had already felt they had been deserted by a friend on some occasion. We talked about what it means to be a real friend and to stay around through difficult times. I challenged each of them to be a real friend *and* to be prepared for disappearing friends.

22

Quality-People Blessing

 I firmly believe the truth of what one of my former professors used to challenge us, his students, with: "The people you meet and the books you read today will determine the person you are five years from now." That statement reminds me to intentionally pursue meeting excellent people and to challenge myself with great literature.

As a father, it encourages me to push for these things for my children as well.

When Kari was nine years old, we were invited by the Fellowship of Christian Athletes to a breakfast honoring the Nebraska and Tennessee football teams, the teams who would face each other at that year's Fiesta Bowl. Hundreds of people sat around tables with football players from the two teams.

We were privileged to have Brook Berringer, former starting quarterback for Nebraska, sitting at our table. Brook hadn't been chosen as starter that year, but he had handled his demotion with an incredible attitude. The biggest factor playing into his positive outlook on his situation was his faith in Jesus Christ. Brook shared with the table that he had realized that there was much more to life than being a starting quarterback, and he was unashamed in sharing his faith. Brook was very kind to Kari, and she still remembers to this day the experience of meeting him. (None of us who had sat with him that morning realized that in fewer than six months, Brook's life would come to an abrupt end when the private plane he was piloting crashed.)

As much as possible, I make an effort to arrange for Kari and Laura to meet people of great character or accomplishment. I want my daughters to meet people like Brook Berringer, who was not only an incredible athlete but also an incredible example of what it means to serve Christ with your life.

Bring people of great character into your son or daughter's life. Is there a teacher who your child really enjoys? Could you invite them to your home for dinner? Could you set up a meeting with a pastor at your church? Do you have coworkers who really impress you with their work ethic? The people you introduce to your child don't have to be famous people, but they *should* be people who walk through life with integrity and use their abilities to benefit others. Those are the sort of people you want your son or daughter to rub shoulders with. Make an effort to introduce your son or daughter to people of great character so that your child can learn valuable lessons from not only you but also others you choose to surround them with.

23

Gold-Medal Blessing

 Unfortunately, we often acknowledge negative behavior much more than we do positive behavior. Have you ever had a boss who you felt like only noticed you when you did something wrong? Did you feel like all of the time you spent doing what was right didn't really matter? We have a great opportunity to encourage our children when we see them demonstrate exceptional character, to see and acknowledge the potential in them for impacting their world in meaningful ways.

Cindy and I instituted the Medal of Merit award for outstanding courage, character, accomplishments, or caring acts. The medal was nothing more than a plastic gold medal I picked up at the party store, but the ceremony that accompanied it was what made it special. Kari and Laura knew nothing about the medals until we first presented Kari with one.

Kari and several other freshmen were chosen to be part of the varsity cheer squad at their high school. While this was certainly a boost for each girl's self-esteem, it was also a lot of stress and responsibility heaped onto them. The varsity squad was expected to cheer year-round for the various sports, sometimes as many as six times a week. While it was certainly challenging, Kari worked really hard to find a balance as she juggled the newness of high school, the demands of cheer, and the rigor of honors classes. We watched as she demonstrated exceptional faithfulness, effort, and endurance.

When the year reached an especially stressful point, I decided it would be more than appropriate to award Kari the Medal of Merit. I presented her with the medal and spoke words of encouragement to her of how proud I was of her courage in the face of great stress and even adversity. The three-minute conversation didn't require much effort from me, but it spoke volumes to Kari, who hung the medal from her mirror for years afterward.

Make a point to acknowledge with some level of ceremony the outstanding acts of good character that you see your son or daughter commit. Making a big deal about your child's character is worth doing, and it will bless your child as they see that you believe they are capable of great things and that God has great things in store for them. And remember how this book began: "Every child in every home deserves to know that someone is crazy about them." Make sure that the gold medal doesn't just go to the oldest or the fastest or the smartest child. Look for ways to bless each child in ways that reflect the high value you see in each one's life.

24

Number-One-Fan Blessing

 When I was growing up, basketball was my least favorite sport. I played football, so I ran into people on purpose. In basketball, there are things called fouls, things that indicate you messed up because you ran into someone on purpose. I could never quite make that mental change. In fact, the only sport I disliked more

than basketball was cheerleading, which I didn't even consider to be a real sport.

So, as God would have it, one of my daughters developed a passion for basketball and the other, a passion for cheerleading. And remember, my goal was to bless them both.

Over the years, I have talked to so many men who have been stretched in this way as their sons or daughters became enthusiasts about the sports or activities they (the fathers) deemed illegitimate or a waste of time in their youth. But rather than give your son or daughter grief about their choice of sport or hobby, give honor instead. Instead of stepping away, step towards what they value. That's a great way to bless them.

Biblically, the word *honor* refers to something heavy or weighty—gold for example would be weighty. I wouldn't have associated gold with cheerleading, but Kari chose cheerleading as her favorite sport. So I got a new favorite sport. Even though I deeply disliked basketball, when Laura chose it as her favorite sport, I got a second, new favorite sport. I watched my girls work hard and push themselves physically to be an asset to their respective teams. And I learned to appreciate the efforts put in by the athletes devoted to both cheer and basketball. I encouraged my girls along the way to be the best they could be, and while I was certainly striving to bless them, I can say without a doubt that the Lord blessed me as I humbled myself to be a fan of cheerleading and basketball (at least when my girls were involved!).

One last thought on blessing your child by being their biggest fan: It also means that you bless your son or daughter even if they don't seek to be good at what you were good at. I went to high school with a baseball player who was simply outstanding. In fact, by our senior year, he was a Topps baseball card high school All-American. That's the top selection of all high school All-American teams for baseball. And he never played one minute of baseball after he graduated high school. He wasn't injured. And yes, he was offered a college scholarship *and* a pro contract(!), both of which he turned down. But his father had pushed and shoved him so hard to be him—the dad, a former baseball player—that when my friend got out on his own, he wouldn't even pick up a mitt.

Blessing a child doesn't mean they become you. So look for ways to be a fan of your child, not someone who pushes them into a sport that gives you a chance to relive the past.

25

Stick-to-Your-Commitments Blessing

 Just as it is important for you to get behind whatever sport your son or daughter chooses, it's important that you teach your son or daughter to stick for a season to the sport they've committed themselves to. While childhood and adolescence are certainly times to experience different things and evaluate interests, bailing midseason should not be an option. Your son or daughter needs to learn the value of sticking to commitments, and sports is a great training ground for this.

We had the "quitting is not an option" talk with both of our daughters before they committed to things, and one season in particular, not quitting was especially hard for Laura. Laura had joined a baseball team only to discover that all of the other players had been playing together for at least a couple of years. She quickly felt left out, not only from the social aspect of the team, but even while playing the game. Time and time again, the other girls would demonstrate preference for familiar teammates as they deliberately avoided throwing the ball to Laura or supporting her on the field. She became so frustrated that she asked us in tears if she could quit. We stuck to our guns, and she played the rest of the season, but it was tough. Still, years later, there are times when she will say to us, "Thanks for making me gut that out with baseball. It's helped me know that there are times, like in a bad job, when for a season, you just have to tough things out." You will bless your son or daughter by holding to this rule, as you set them up to take their commitments in life seriously and to follow through with what they say they will do.

26

Knowing-Your-Strengths Blessing

 One of the ways that I am most passionate about fathers blessing their children is for dads to champion an effort to help their kids understand their strengths.

Included here is the LOGB® Personal Strengths Assessment (That's short for Lion/Otter/Golden Retriever/Beaver!) I created years ago. This is basically a quick quiz to help you determine your God-given strengths and those of your son or daughter as well.

First, make a copy of the assessment for yourself and for each child. As you prepare to take the quiz, be aware that this is a first-guess assessment. So go with your initial response, rather than overanalyzing every word or phrase. Starting with the L box circle every word or phrase (there are fourteen of them) in the box that describes you as a person and circle the sentence "Let's do it now!" After you've worked through the L box, then do the same for the O, G, and B boxes.

L

Takes charge
Determined
Assertive
Firm
Enterprising
Competitive
Enjoys challenges

Bold
Purposeful
Decision maker
Leader
Goal-driven
Self-reliant
Adventurous

"Let's do it now!"

Double the number circled _____

O

Takes risks
Visionary
Motivator
Energetic
Very verbal
Promoter
Avoids details

Fun-loving
Likes variety
Enjoys change
Creative
Group-oriented
Mixes easily
Optimistic

"Trust me! It'll work out!"

Double the number circled _____

G

Loyal	Adaptable
Nondemanding	Sympathetic
Even keel	Thoughtful
Avoids conflict	Nurturing
Enjoys routine	Patient
Dislikes change	Tolerant
Deep relationships	Good listener

"Let's keep things the way they are."

Double the number circled _____

B

Deliberate	Discerning
Controlled	Detailed
Reserved	Analytical
Predictable	Inquisitive
Practical	Precise
Orderly	Persistent
Factual	Scheduled

"How was it done in the past?"

Double the number circled _____

STRENGTHS ASSESSMENT CHART

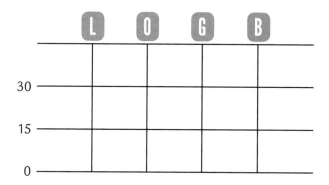

Example:

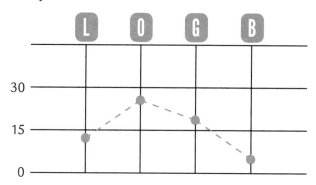

Now you're ready to score your quiz. Start with the L box. At the very bottom of the box is a place for the total score. So in the L box, count up all the words and phrases you circled and include the circled sentence at the bottom of the box. Let's say you circled 6 words and/or phrases and the "Let's do it now!" for a total of 7 circles. Now double your score, which would be 14 (that's 7 x 2 = 14). Put 14 where the total score is to go. Go on through the O, G, and B boxes, counting up all the circles and doubling that number for the total score in each. Let's say your total scores were 14 in L, 26 in O, 18 in G, and 4 in B. Take those total scores and mark the appropriate spots on the graph. So on the L line, you'd mark 14; on the O, you'd put a mark roughly where 26 would be, etc. Now connect the dots. What you'll have is a visual graph of your unique, God-given strengths.

After you've taken your assessment, have your son or daughter take the quiz to figure out their strengths. Depending on their age, you can help with the vocabulary of course, but as much as possible, let them do their own work. When they've finished, double the number of circles in each box, and plot the total scores on the graph. You'll get to see their graph, and this knowledge of how they view themselves—what their God-given strengths are—can be a great tool in blessing your child!

As you'll see, the graph and what it says about your child will give you a means of affirming your son or daughter by highlighting the strengths you see in them, and you will have a better picture of how they see you.

My friend Gary Smalley and I wrote an entire book about this assessment called *The Two Sides of Love*, but let me give you a snapshot of what L, O, G, and B each look like.

If the highest score on the assessment is in the L box, then you are a Lion. Lions tend to be charge-ahead, take-charge people. They are often the boss (or they think they are). They're good at making quick decisions and can become impatient with anything that gets in their way (like red lights!). They're great leaders who get things done but may need to be better listeners—particularly if their G-box scores are very low.

If you scored highest in the O box, then you are an Otter. Otters are what we call "parties waiting to happen!" They are fun-loving and very verbal, and they usually know hundreds of people—they just don't remember everyone's name! They're great at starting things and creating new things, but they tend not to be thoroughly organized; for example, they can start to balance the checkbook but not finish the task. (And in some cases, they just switch banks to find out their balance!) Otters are the ones with a sock room rather than a meticulously kept sock drawer. They're a lot of fun, but sometimes they need to be more serious or organized to get things done.

Those with the highest G-box scores are Golden Retrievers. They are team players, very consistent, warm, and fuzzy; and they want everyone to feel part of the family. They can often have trouble saying no, because they don't want to disappoint anyone. For example, Golden Retrievers tend to buy eighteen to twenty boxes of Girl Scout cookies every year, because it's almost genetically impossible for a Golden Retriever to say one small but very important word: "No!" Despite this, they're great listeners, counselors, and encouragers. But sometimes, they are so soft on people that they can be too soft on problems as well. They have a tendency to struggle with discipline and often push off a problem ("Oh, it'll go away").

Finally, guess what's on the class ring at MIT. Or at Cal Tech. (Two of our finest engineering schools in the country). Well, if your score is highest in the B box, then you are a Beaver, just like at MIT or Cal Tech! Beavers are organized, detailed, and precise. They like to finish things they start (Otters like to start things and start more things and start more things). Beavers enjoy systems of accomplishing things and are great at detailed work. Because of their attention to even the smallest things, they may be critical of others and can be really hard on themselves. And they often want the string with the ball on the end to be hanging from the ceiling in the garage, because the car needs to go right . . . there!

Once you and your children have completed your assessments, take some time to discuss the results. Who are the Lions in your family? The Otters? The Golden Retrievers? The Beavers? Talk with your son or daughter about how they see themselves and how you see them. Talk about how you see yourself and how they see you.

It may be that you see each other very differently than you see yourselves. Give your children examples of the times you see them act certain ways and let them give you examples of your behavior as well. Do your best to focus on the strengths, rather than the weaknesses, but you certainly can make plans for how you can work to better understand and encourage one another. Seeing each other's strengths is a powerful means of blessing. It's a way to both attach high value and picture a special future for each child as you encourage them with how you see God using their personality and how you envision he will use it in the future.

While there will probably be one of the personality profiles that you feel most strongly fits your son or daughter (or yourself), it is important to note that everyone has a blend of the personalities, so some traits of each profile may fit your son or daughter. Taking time to be a student of your son and daughter and learning more about them is crucial to being able to bless them according to their personality (plus, as children are growing, their personalities may take dramatic turns!). Below we will look at some specific ways you might consider to bless your child according to their particular personality, whether they be a Lion, Otter, Golden Retriever, or Beaver.

27

Lion Blessing

 If you discover that your son or daughter is a Lion, one way to bless them that speaks specifically to their personality is to have a goal-setting session with them and regularly revisit their goals with them. Sit down and talk about what they want to accomplish in the next semester at school, and ask if there is any way you can better help them reach their goals. Set a date to revisit the goals, and when the target date for completion comes, encourage them about the goals they have met and don't give as much attention to the goals that may have been missed.

28

Otter Blessing

 If your son or daughter is an Otter, I would highly recommend your letting them help host social events in your home. Make your home the hang-out place for your son or daughter and their friends. When you create an atmosphere where others feel welcome, your young Otter will be blessed by the opportunities to have fun and be the natural social chatterbox that they are. Make a point to ask your son or daughter what you can do to help them enjoy having friends over. Plus when you make your house the playground, you can be more aware of who your child is hanging out with and what activities they are involved in.

29

Golden Retriever Blessing

 If your son or daughter is a Golden Retriever, make an extra effort to spend regular one-on-one time with them. Go to their favorite restaurant, ice cream place, or store. Read a book with them and spend time talking about it. Golden Retrievers love deep conversation and close relationships. Cultivating with your son or daughter a close relationship in which they feel comfortable talking to you and valued by you will bless them beyond measure.

30

Beaver Blessing

 If your son or daughter is a Beaver, a blessing to them may be to let them have some of their own space and some rules and/or boundaries that protect this space. Perhaps allow them to organize their room however they want and to establish reasonable rules for entering the space, such as knocking before coming in, requesting to borrow items, etc. While some of these may be common rules of courtesy that everyone in the house is expected to follow, making sure that your Beaver is comfortable and feels respected is important. Take some time to praise them for the strengths you see in them, and give them time to think about what boundaries they might like to help protect their space. And make sure you compliment them, not just for what they do (which is usually top quality), but for who they are as well. And especially let them know they don't lose your blessing when they fall short. (They're so hard on themselves.)

LET THE BLESSING BEGIN

THAT'S THIRTY PRACTICAL ways you can pass on the blessing to your son or daughter in the days to come. The blessing is so powerful, it can affect a child for a lifetime. It is my prayer that you received the blessing in your own home as a child, but even if you didn't, know that the Lord rescues, redeems, and brings you his blessing through the grace of Jesus Christ. The blessing of a father—your blessing—is incredibly powerful. You can be that man, the one who leaves a legacy of the blessing in your child's life. May your children be blessed when you do.

I'm praying for you as you embark on a journey to bless your son or daughter. Keep your eyes fixed on the Lord. Seek him earnestly and he will honor you as you seek to bless your family. Let me close with a prayer for you as you embark on a mission to bring the blessing home to your family:

Father God,

Thank you for the father who is reading this and who desires to bless his children.

Lord, I pray that he himself experienced the blessing.

I pray Lord, that he knows what it means to be touched in a way that expresses care, tenderness, and strength.

I pray that he has heard words spoken to him that communicate that he is of great worth, that you have created him uniquely, and that you have remarkable plans for him.

*I sincerely hope that he has received the
blessing from his own father, but, Lord,
if he didn't, I pray that he will embrace the
blessing that you bestow upon him.*

*As he strives to then bless
his sons and daughters,
may those young men and women that
you have placed in his care grow to be a
generation who loves you deeply and serves
you with a passion as they know
that they were created for a purpose.*

*We love you, Lord Jesus,
and trust you to do beyond
what we could ever ask or imagine.*

In your Son's precious name we do pray.

Amen.

Bring the Blessing to Your Home

A spouse's or a parent's approval affects the way people view themselves. You can give your spouse and/or your children the gift of unconditional acceptance the Bible calls the blessing. This set of four short booklets is packed with tips on what the blessing is, and each booklet gives 30 ideas on how to give it to those around you. Even if you didn't get the blessing as a child, you can learn to give it to others.

Author John Trent is a Christian psychologist and co-author of the million-copy bestselling book, *The Blessing*. He shares his own story of his father's abandonment, and how he learned to give the blessing to his children.

Paperback, 112 pages, 4.5 x 6.5 x .25 inches

30 Ways a Father Can Bless His Children
ISBN 9781628622775

30 Ways a Mother Can Bless Her Children
ISBN 9781628622805

30 Ways a Husband Can Bless His Wife
ISBN 9781628622836

30 Ways a Wife Can Bless Her Husband
ISBN 9781628622867